GW01605574

for the children of
Southmere First School
with love

British Library Cataloguing in Publication Data
Swindells, Robert Edward
The Weather-Clerk
I. Title
823'.9'1J PZ7.S9818

ISBN 0-340-23904-2 (cased)
ISBN 0-340-34619-1 (paperbound)

First published 1979 (cased)
First published 1983 (paperbound)

Published by Hodder and Stoughton Children's Books,
a division of Hodder and Stoughton Ltd, Mill Road,
Dunton Green, Sevenoaks, Kent TN13 2YJ

Printed in Great Britain by
Springbourne Press Limited, Basildon, Essex

The Weather~Clerk

Story by Robert Swindells
Illustrated by Petula Stone

HODDER AND STOUGHTON
LONDON SYDNEY AUCKLAND TORONTO

mon
9
june
Jane

The sun streamed in through the classroom window. Mr Partridge looked at it and rubbed his hands. "I hope it's like this next Wednesday," he said.

"Why, Mr Partridge?" said Anna.

"Because," said Mr Partridge, "next Wednesday is our class outing."

Somebody went "Oooh!" and all the children began talking at once.

"Where are we going?" yelled Terry Leach.

Mr Partridge frowned at him, "We are going to the airport to watch the planes," he said. "If we behave ourselves in the meantime and don't bellow across the classroom like a cow with toothache. And afterwards we shall have a picnic lunch in the park, where there are swings and things."

At half-past three, Anna ran down to the crossing. Mrs Puxon the lollipop lady was there. Anna told her about the outing.

R. COUGH
P. CHO
STOP

"You'll have a lovely day," said Mrs Puxon, "if it keeps fine."

"Yes," said Anna. "But what if it doesn't?"

"Ah, well," replied Mrs Puxon thoughtfully, "I reckon you want a word with the Weather-Clerk."

"The who?" said Anna.

"The Weather-Clerk," said Mrs Puxon. "He's the one who decides the sort of days we get."

Anna couldn't tell if the lollipop lady was kidding.

"Where does he live?" she asked suspiciously.

"Inkermann Street, love," smiled Mrs Puxon. "Number one, right in the middle of the city. Take him some flowers. He's a miserable old so-and-so, but he likes a few flowers, the Weather-Clerk does."

Anna ran home. After tea she said, "I'm off out to play, Mum."

E.OFFLE
OPEN

"All right love," said her Mum.

Anna went into the garden and picked some flowers. She made them into a bunch and hurried off along the street.

At the end of the street she saw a policeman. He was looking in a shop-window.

"Excuse me," said Anna. "Please could you tell me where Inkermann Street is?"

"Inkermann Street?" said the policeman. "Now let me see." He stroked his chin a minute, thinking. "Oh yes, I know the place. Just a minute." He took out his notebook and a pencil. "I'll draw you a plan." He drew in the notebook, then tore out the page and gave it to Anna.

"There," he said. "This is where we are, right? You just follow the dotted line I've drawn and you'll be there in no time."

Anna thanked him and hurried on, with the plan in one hand and the flowers in the other.

She had just turned the first corner when it began to rain. It was not like ordinary rain.

This rain began so suddenly, and fell so hard that Anna knew the Weather-Clerk was doing it on purpose. She leapt into a doorway. The street was all swirling water and gurgling drains. Then, as suddenly as it had started, the rain stopped and the sun came out again. Anna left the doorway and went on, dodging between the puddles.

"You can't stop me, Weather-Clerk," she whispered.

She turned the next corner. There was a roaring, whistling sound. Down the street came whirling sheets of old newspaper, crisp-packets and fallen leaves.

The wind was so strong it knocked her over and sent her rolling along the pavement with all the litter. She rolled up against a lamp-post and clung on to it with her eyes closed. After a minute, the wind was gone. Anna picked herself up, found her flowers in a corner, and went on.

"You can't stop me, Weather-Clerk," she whispered.

The next moment, Anna found herself in the middle of a thick, grey fog. She stopped.

Everything was hidden. There was only a quiet, smoky greyness with shadows in it. She began to walk, very slowly, with one hand out in front of her. She was scared.

All at once she came out into bright sunshine, and there on a wall in front of her was a sign that said "Inkermann Street".

"You can't stop me, Weather-Clerk," laughed Anna.

She easily found number one, and knocked on the door. It was opened by a thin old man in slippers. He had a bald head and big round glasses.

60°
61°
61°
64°
65°
VOL
FoG

"Oh!" he said gruffly. "So you got here did you, through all that bad weather?" Anna nodded, and held out the flowers.

"I've brought you these," she smiled. "You *are* the Weather-Clerk, aren't you?"

"That's me," said the Weather-Clerk. He took the flowers and sniffed at them.

"Hm! Nice. Well, you'd better come in, hadn't you?"

Anna followed the old man and found herself in the oddest room she had ever seen. Every wall was covered with clocks, dials, knobs and screens. There were tables with strange machines on them.

Anna just stood and stared.

SPECIAL EVENTS
magical mystery tours
day trips
weddings and funerals
nature rambles
sports
vicar's tea party FOG
Brownies seaside trip
W.V.S. windy
Southmere first school RAIN!
All rained off!
botany class
tree felling club lots of rain!
Man. utd-Home win!
Hockey club abandoned
Rowing club
Teddy bears picnic
Operatic society-FOG
amateur dramatics - Henry V

"Well?" said the Weather-Clerk. "What do you want?"

"Can you make sunny days?" asked Anna.

"Of course I can!" snapped the Weather-Clerk. "I can make any sort of day I like."

"Well," said Anna. "Will you make it sunny next Wednesday, please?"

"Why?" the Weather-Clerk asked.

"Because we have our outing next Wednesday," Anna told him.

"Outing?" said the Weather-Clerk, sharply. He went over to a big chart on the wall. On the chart were details of weddings, outings, picnics and garden parties. The old man ran his finger down the list. "Oh yes, here it is. Southmere First School. Class outing." He ran his fingers along the line.

"Rain!" he said.

"Oh!" gasped Anna. "Why?"

HAIL
RAIN
MIXTURE

The Weather-Clerk chuckled nastily.
"I usually make it rain on people's outings," he said. "More fun."
"Well *I* don't think so!" exclaimed Anna.
"I think it's mean and cruel!"
The Weather-Clerk pressed a button.
"Watch," he chuckled.
A screen lit up. It was a picture of the park. People were sitting on the grass. The Weather-Clerk went over to one of his machines and flicked a switch.
The machine began to turn.
In the park, hailstones fell. The people got up and ran, holding things over their heads. They ran along the path with the hailstones bouncing all round them. The Weather-Clerk laughed so much he had to sit down.

Anna glared at him.

"You're just a mean, nasty old man!" she cried.

"I wish I hadn't brought you the flowers."

The Weather-Clerk stopped laughing. He switched off the Hail Machine, stood up and stamped his foot.

"Nobody ever comes to see me," he said.

"I've lived here all my life, and I don't think I've had more than six visitors in all that time."

He began to walk up and down, frowning.

"It's not fair. If the weather's bad, everybody blames me. But nobody ever says, 'Good old Weather-Clerk' when it's fine, do they?"

He sat down again.

"It's boring, you know, being alone all the time. That's why I like to have a bit of fun with my machines. They're my only friends, these machines."

Anna sat down, too, and looked at him.

"Perhaps," she said, "if you stopped

playing mean tricks with your machines, people would visit you sometimes. I would, anyway."

"Huh!" said the Weather-Clerk. "No you wouldn't. You only came because you want a fine day next Wednesday. If you get it, I'll never see you again."

"You will!" cried Anna. "Try it and see."

The old man looked at her. Suddenly he seemed rather sad.

"Do you really think people might come to see me?" he asked.

Anna nodded her head.

"I'm sure they would. And I know I would. I'd like to see the rest of your machines."

"Would you?" said the Weather-Clerk.

"Really?"

Anna smiled and nodded. She thought she saw the beginning of a smile in the old man's eyes, too. He got up.

"Come on then," he said. "I'll show them to you now."

Anna followed him round the room. She saw the Wind-Engine, the Sun-Dial and the Cloud-Maker.

The Cloud-Maker was like a candy-floss machine. The Weather-Clerk set it spinning, dipped in a stick, and wound some cloud on to it for Anna.

It tasted grey, and Anna pulled a face.

The Weather-Clerk was definitely smiling now.

"Would you like to stay for tea?" he asked.

"What about next Wednesday?" demanded Anna.

The old man winked. "Oh," he said.

"I expect I can fix something up for you. After all, you did bring me some flowers."

So Anna stayed for tea. There were fog-rolls, rainburgers, sun-buns and apple-snow. Then it was time to go.

"Thank you for the tea," said Anna. "And for the sunshine next Wednesday."

"You're welcome," said the Weather-Clerk.

"Don't forget to come and see me again, will you? I'm thinking of bringing out coloured snow, you know." He waved goodbye and Anna walked home through the little streets.

Roller Coa
PRIVATE
EFH 147F

And when Wednesday came, it was warm and sunny all day. The children played on the swings and rolled about in the grass till teatime. Then they climbed into the coach to go home. Terry Leach flopped down next to Anna with jam all round his mouth.

"What a smashing day!" he said.

"You wait till next year," smiled Anna. "I bet we'll have coloured snow."

P. STONE